No Chicken, No Trees

Donald Brown

NO CHICKEN, NO TREES

Paperback edition / June 2018

Copyright (c) 2018 by Donald Brown

Library of Congress Catalog Card Number: On File

Author e-mail: donnieb1087@gmail.com

This novel is a work of fiction. Any references to real people, event, business, organization, or locales are intended only to give the fiction a sense of reality and authenticity. Names, characters, place, and incidents are the product of the author's imagination or used fictitiously. Any resemblance to actual persons, living or dead, events, or locales, is entirely coincidental.

All rights reserved. No parts of this book may be used or reproduced in any manner whatsoever without written permission from the author, except in case of brief quotations embodied in critical articles and reviews.

ISBN 978-1-7326542-0-4

Published simultaneously in the US and Canada

PRINTED IN THE UNITED STATES OF AMERICA

Rumble, rumble in the tummy, baby Ethan says he's hungry.

Mommy Cheryl hears his cry and gets him set for dinnertime.

The mashed potatoes and blueberry muffin surely are healthy and look awfully scrumptious.

Baby Ethan looks so happy; he turns around and smiles at daddy.

He takes a moment to look back at his plate but notices something that isn't so great...

A big sloppy piece of meat and puffy stuff that's ever so green.

Mommy tells Ethan that those aren't trees; it's actually a vegetable called broccoli.

But Ethan won't budge; he dislikes what he sees so he tells them again, "No chicken, no trees."

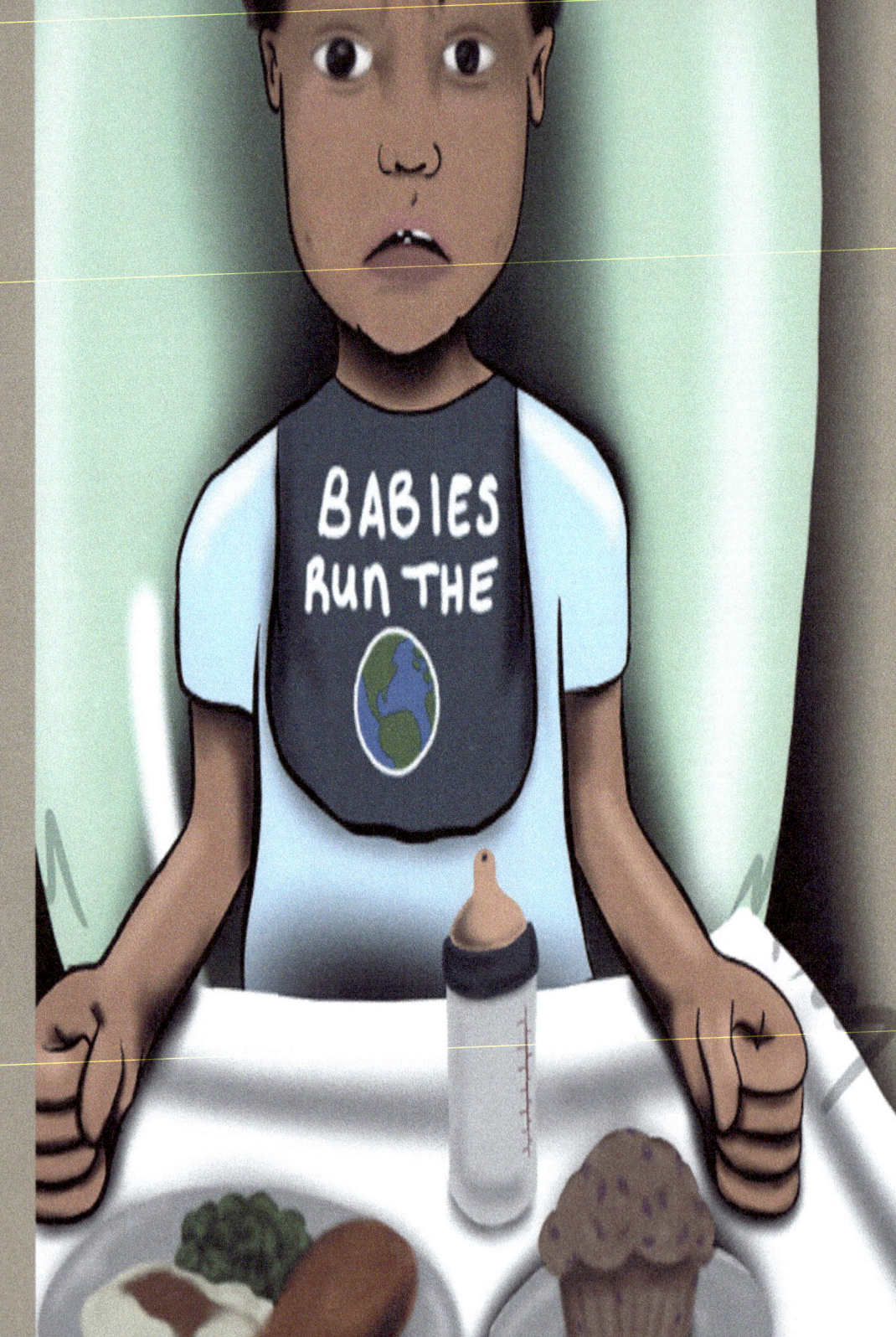

Mommy's displeased and daddy is too.
What on Earth are they going to do?

The food's getting cold since Ethan won't eat, but daddy thinks he has a trick up his sleeve.

He chops up the chicken then seasons the veggies and tells baby Ethan it's good for his belly.

Ethan's not sure if daddy is right, but something is telling him, "Just take a bite!"

He opens his mouth and gives it a shot.
He chews all his food and swallows the slop.

But to his surprise baby Ethan is pleased, "I like it, I like it," he says as he beams.

Mommy and daddy are filled with joy.
Ethan is growing into a big boy!

Now the food is gone; time for Ethan to sleep, but he has one thing to say first, "More chicken, more trees... please."

www.ingramcontent.com/pod-product-compliance
Lightning Source LLC
Chambersburg PA
CBHW040045100526
44584CB00033BA/4445